CW01064481

Original title:

Circle of Friends: Expanding Your Social Bonds

Author: Paula Raudsepp

ISBN HARDBACK: 978-9916-89-043-1

ISBN PAPERBACK: 978-9916-89-044-8

ISBN EBOOK: 978-9916-89-045-5

The Ties That Enrich

Threads of memories hold us tight,
In laughter's echo, hearts take flight.
Through storms we walk, through sun we play,
Each moment cherished, come what may.

In silence shared, our spirits blend,
Every whisper, a bond we mend.
With open hands, we face the day,
Together stronger, come what may.

Woven Together

In a tapestry of dreams we weave,
Our hopes and fears we both believe.
Each stitch a story, rich and true,
A canvas painted in shades of you.

With every thread, a promise made,
In the fabric of life, we aren't afraid.
Hand in hand, we journey far,
Guided always by our star.

Cadence of Companionship

With every step, a rhythm grows,
A dance of hearts where love bestows.
In laughter's song, we softly sway,
Together moving, come what may.

Through life's parade, we find the beat,
In shared moments, our hearts repeat.
Bound by trust, our spirits sing,
In harmony, we find our spring.

The Light We Share

In shadowed paths, your light will shine,
A beacon bright, forever mine.
Through darkest nights, we walk as one,
With guiding stars, our journey begun.

Your laughter glows in dusky hue,
In every dawn, I see you true.
Together bright, we break the dark,
Illuminating every spark.

Unity in Diversity

Colors blend, side by side,
Voices rise, far and wide.
Different paths, one we tread,
Harmony in words unsaid.

Cultures rich, stories shared,
Each unique, yet all cared.
Hand in hand, we stand as one,
Underneath the same warm sun.

The sky holds each star's light,
Through the day and into night.
Together strong, we pave the way,
In unity, we'll forever stay.

Webs of Connection

Threads of silver, golden lines,
Intertwined, our fate aligns.
Every soul a vibrant thread,
In this tapestry we thread.

Silent whispers, hearts that beat,
In the shadows, we meet.
Connections growing, roots that bind,
In every heart, love you will find.

Voices echo, stories told,
In each strand, memories unfold.
Together woven, never apart,
We share a sacred, beating heart.

The Ties That Bind

Invisible threads, strong yet fine,
Hold us close, in love entwined.
Through storms fierce and skies so blue,
These ties of friendship, ever true.

Shared laughter echoes in the air,
Moments cherished, always rare.
When we falter, lift us high,
In each other's strength, we fly.

Even when the miles divide,
In our hearts, we still reside.
These bonds unbroken, never frayed,
In every memory we've made.

Embracing New Horizons

Morning sun paints skies anew,
With open hearts, we greet the view.
Change is here, with gentle light,
Inviting dreams to take their flight.

Waves of courage, winds of chance,
In the unknown, we find our dance.
Each step forward, brave and bold,
Stories waiting to unfold.

Boundless futures, paths unwritten,
Hearts ablaze, ambitions smitten.
Together chasing dreams that rise,
Embracing life, we touch the skies.

Echoes of Friendship

In laughter's glow, we share our dreams,
With whispered hopes, like flowing streams.
Together we rise, through thick and thin,
A bond unbroken, we always win.

Through stormy nights, our spirits soar,
In silent moments, we trust and explore.
The path of life, with hands entwined,
In every heartbeat, our joys aligned.

Memories linger, in twilight's hue,
Reminding us of the love so true.
With gentle echoes, they softly call,
Friendship's embrace, the greatest gift of all.

Hand in Hand

Side by side, we face the dawn,
With every step, our fears are gone.
Hand in hand, we chase the light,
Together, we'll conquer every night.

Through the valleys, and the hills,
Each moment shared, our heartbeats thrill.
In the dance of life, we learn to sway,
With every challenge, we find our way.

With trust as our guide, we venture forth,
In the tapestry of dreams, we find our worth.
Hand in hand, we'll build the plan,
In this journey, just understand.

Heart to Heart

In the quiet of our shared space,
We find comfort in every embrace.
Heart to heart, where secrets reside,
In the warmth of love, we safely confide.

Together we breathe, in sync we move,
In the rhythm of life, we find our groove.
With every pulse, our spirits sing,
A melody of joy that kindness can bring.

Through trials faced, our hopes ignite,
In the glow of friendship, we shine bright.
With an open heart, we will start,
To weave a tale that won't depart.

Cultivating Companionship

In gardens where our laughter grows,
We plant the seeds of friendship's prose.
With tender care, we watch them bloom,
In the light of love, they chase the gloom.

As seasons change, we nurture trust,
In every moment, we learn we must.
Cultivating bonds that time won't fray,
Together we thrive, come what may.

In shared stories and whispered dreams,
We craft a life like silver streams.
With hands together, we tend the heart,
In this precious space, we never part.

Resonance of Hearts

In the silence, our hearts converse,
A harmony woven, a universe.
With every heartbeat, a song unfolds,
In the resonance of love, we're bold.

Through every trial, we find our way,
Echoing laughter, brightening the day.
In connection deep, our spirits blend,
In the tapestry of time, our stories mend.

A rhythm that dances, in perfect time,
Together we rise, as we climb.
With souls aligned, we'll never part,
In the symphony of life, we're art.

Spheres of Sweetness

In gardens where the blossoms bloom,
Honey drips from nature's loom.
Sunset paints the skies in gold,
Each moment shared, a story told.

Flavors whisper, warm and bright,
In the quiet of the night.
Joy and laughter intertwine,
A sip of love, a strawberry wine.

Breezes carry scents so rare,
In a world beyond compare.
Each taste a dance, a sweet embrace,
Together in this sacred space.

Waves of sugar on the tongue,
Life's sweet melody is sung.
In every bite, a blissful thrill,
Moments cherished, hearts to fill.

Embracing the Unexpected

Beneath the stars, the night unfolds,
A story waiting to be told.
Twists and turns along the way,
In shadows bright, we find our play.

Surprises dance within the breeze,
Rustling leaves and bending trees.
Every challenge, a hidden gift,
The heart takes flight, begins to lift.

In the chaos, beauty glows,
From unknown paths, our courage grows.
We meet the dawn with open arms,
Embracing life, its wondrous charms.

Through winding roads, we chase the light,
With every step, we crave the height.
In the unplanned, we find our song,
In every moment, we belong.

The Mosaic of Together

Fragments of life, colors collide,
In this tapestry, we abide.
Each thread a story, rich and deep,
In harmony, our dreams we keep.

Hands entwined, we build anew,
Every shade a vibrant hue.
In laughter shared, in silence met,
A bond like this, we won't forget.

Through storms we stand, unwavering,
In love's embrace, we are braving.
With every heartbeat, we create,
A masterpiece, it's never late.

In the breaking, we find our way,
Together strong, come what may.
Unified, we face the strife,
Becoming art, this precious life.

Windows to New Worlds

Through glass and frame, horizons gleam,
Each view invites a waking dream.
Vistas vast and skies so wide,
In every glance, new worlds abide.

Open your heart, let visions flow,
Beyond the walls, let wonder grow.
The journeys start with just one gaze,
Into the night, through twilight haze.

Windows wide to realms unknown,
In every sight, a seed is sown.
Let curiosity ignite the flame,
With every look, we'll never be the same.

Chasing sunsets, stars align,
With every look, our spirits shine.
In uncharted lands, we take flight,
Windows to worlds, bursting with light.

The Circle of Kindred Spirits

In twilight's glow, we gather near,
Whispers of hearts, warm and clear.
With laughter shared, our worries cease,
Each moment lived, a thread of peace.

Bound by love, through thick and thin,
In the darkest times, we still win.
Together we stand, our spirits rise,
Underneath the vast, starlit skies.

Through trials faced, we find our way,
Guided by light, come what may.
With hands entwined, we face the storm,
In each other's arms, we're safe and warm.

Every story told, a bond so tight,
In the depths of night, we find our light.
With kindness sewn into our dreams,
Together forever, or so it seems.

As seasons change and time moves fast,
The memories we make are meant to last.
In circling arms, we're never apart,
Forever connected, heart to heart.

Bonds That Strengthen

In the tapestry of life, we weave,
Threads of friendship that never leave.
Through laughter and tears, we'll always stand,
Supporting each other, hand in hand.

From quiet whispers to joyful cries,
In every moment, the spirit flies.
With every challenge that comes our way,
Together we're stronger, come what may.

Each promise made, a treasure held,
In the storms of life, our spirits swelled.
With every heartbeat, every sigh,
Our bonds grow deeper, reaching the sky.

In the quiet hours and bustling days,
Our friendship shines in countless ways.
Through the echoes of time, we remain,
In the strength of love, we feel no pain.

When shadows linger, and doubts creep in,
With faith and trust, we always win.
For in this world, so fast and wide,
Our bonds are the anchors, our hearts collide.

Colorful Horizons

Painted skies of orange and blue,
With every sunrise, a world anew.
The colors dance in joyful play,
Promising hope for a brighter day.

With every horizon, a story unfolds,
In shades of copper, and glimmers of gold.
The sunsets whisper secrets untold,
In the warmth of light, our dreams behold.

Beneath the arch of the endless night,
Stars sprinkle dreams like shards of light.
With every twinkle, a wish takes flight,
Under the vastness, we find delight.

As dawn awakens with gentle grace,
We find in each moment, our rightful place.
In nature's canvas, we see It clear,
A world so vivid, we hold so dear.

Together we chase the colors that blend,
In laughter and wonder, around each bend.
With open hearts, we embrace the view,
In the kaleidoscope of life, bright and true.

Symphony of Shared Tales

In the quiet corners, stories ignite,
Whispers of dreams in the still of the night.
Tales of love, of loss, and of pain,
Crafted together, like sunshine and rain.

With every heartbeat, a rhythm flows,
The symphony built from highs and lows.
In the dance of words, our spirits soar,
Each note a story, begging for more.

Gathered around, we listen with care,
Every secret shared, a breath of air.
Through laughter and tears, our bonds grow tight,
In this shared space, we find our light.

For every tale told, a lesson learned,
In the warmth of friendship, our hearts are burned.
Together we write in the book of our years,
A melody woven from joys and tears.

As we turn the pages, each story unfolds,
In the library of life, we cherish the gold.
In unity strong, we face the unknown,
Through the symphony played, we're never alone.

From Hearts to Hands

From hearts that beat with hope,
To hands that reach and mend,
We weave the threads of care,
Together we will stand.

In whispers soft and clear,
We share our dreams at night,
The warmth of love draws near,
Guiding us to the light.

Through trials, we will grow,
In unity, we rise,
For every pain we know,
There's strength in our ties.

With open arms we give,
And take with open minds,
In this place, we shall live,
With hearts and hands aligned.

So let our stories blend,
In a dance both brave and bold,
From hearts to hands we send,
A legacy of gold.

In the Company of Souls

In the company of souls,
We find our place to dwell,
With laughter as our goals,
And stories we will tell.

Through storms and sunny skies,
Together we will thrive,
With every tear and smile,
We keep our love alive.

In moments shared like gold,
We gather strength anew,
In silence, we are bold,
In friendship, we are true.

With eyes that understand,
And hearts that beat as one,
We take each other's hand,
Our journey's just begun.

So here's to us, dear friends,
In this sacred embrace,
In the company that bends,
To elevate our grace.

Gathering Stars

Underneath a velvet sky,
We gather dreams apart,
With wishes whispered high,
And hope to fill our hearts.

The stars, they shine so bright,
Like secrets in the night,
Each twinkle tells a tale,
Of journeys yet to sail.

With every step we take,
We paint our paths in light,
For every choice we make,
We chase the dreams in sight.

Together, hands in hand,
We'll chase the brightest glow,
With courage, we can stand,
And let our spirits flow.

So gather close, my friends,
Let's reach for heights afar,
Our hearts will never end,
While gathering our stars.

A Tapestry of Trust

In the loom of life, we weave,
Threads of courage and care,
With hope and love, believe,
In the stories we share.

Each color tells a tale,
Of moments lost and found,
In joy or in travail,
A bond forever bound.

Together, we will stitch,
Through trials, thick and thin,
With every loving pitch,
We rise and yet begin.

So let us tie each knot,
In faith and understanding,
For what we have is sought,
In a journey so demanding.

In this tapestry so vast,
We find our place and purpose,
Through every die we cast,
In trust, we stand with courage.

Confluence of Shared Dreams

In the silence of night, we gather close,
Casting wishes into the starry pose.
With hopes that weave like threads of gold,
In the tapestry of visions, bold.

We share our fears, our laughter too,
In whispers soft, in vibrant hue.
Hands unite to sketch the skies,
In the confluence where potential lies.

Paths cross in this sacred space,
Where every heartbeat finds its grace.
Together we dream, together we soar,
A symphony of spirits, forevermore.

Under the moon's gentle embrace,
We find the courage, we find our place.
With every dream, a story spins,
In this confluence, where love begins.

Let the rivers of hope entwine,
Flowing gently, forever divine.
In every dream shared, a life ignites,
Together, we paint the endless nights.

The Pulse of Community

In the heart of the town, a rhythm beats,
A melody rich in laughter and treats.
Voices rise, a harmonious song,
In unity we stand, where we belong.

Through trials faced, hand in hand,
We lift each other, together we stand.
In every smile, a bond we create,
The pulse of our hearts, in love innate.

The market buzz, the children play,
Every moment cherished, come what may.
In every corner, stories intertwine,
The pulse of community, a love divine.

Shared meals and memories, woven tight,
In gatherings warm, we find our light.
From morning sun to evening's rest,
In the pulse of togetherness, we are blessed.

With every heartbeat, our spirits rise,
In the tapestry of life, new ties.
Through strength shared, we weave our fate,
The pulse of community, we celebrate.

Blossoming Connections

In the garden where friendships bloom,
Every flower dispels the gloom.
Roots intertwine beneath the ground,
In blossoming connections, love is found.

Petals dance in the warm sunlight,
Colors vibrant, a pure delight.
With every laugh, a bond is grown,
In this space, we are never alone.

Through seasons of change, we steadfast remain,
In every heart, a shared refrain.
With gentle care, our spirits rise,
In blossoming connections, we realize.

Together we reach for the skies above,
With every bloom, a testament of love.
In the embrace of nature's sweet release,
Blossoming connections bring us peace.

Among the branches, we find our way,
In this garden, we choose to stay.
Together, we flourish, forever in bloom,
In the space we create, there's always room.

The Heartbeat of Unity

In the gathering storm, a light begins,
Voices merging, where strength transcends.
In every heartbeat, a common thread,
The heartbeat of unity, rising ahead.

Together we rise, in the face of doubt,
With every challenge, we stand about.
With open hearts and hands held tight,
In unity's warmth, we find our light.

The whispers of hope, the calls of peace,
In our shared journey, we find release.
Through trials faced, we learn to trust,
The heartbeat of unity, a bond robust.

When shadows fall, our spirits shine,
In every moment, your heart is mine.
With every pulse, our dreams unite,
In the heartbeat of unity, we ignite.

With dreams aligned, we forge our way,
Together, unyielding, come what may.
In this rhythm, forever we'll stay,
The heartbeat of unity leads the way.

Widening the Embrace

In the quiet, arms extend,
Gathering warmth, making amends.
Hearts unfold in gentle grace,
Widening the tender embrace.

Memories weave a golden thread,
Moments shared, words unsaid.
Together we rise, side by side,
With love as our faithful guide.

Storms have come and storms will go,
Yet through it all, our roots will grow.
In every laugh, in each soft sigh,
Widening love will never die.

With open hearts, we walk this land,
Creating peace, hand in hand.
In this dance of trust and care,
The world transforms, a love to share.

The Dance of New Encounters

Underneath the moonlit sky,
We twirl and leap, spirits high.
With every step, we share a glance,
In this magic, we take a chance.

New faces spark the fires bright,
An unexpected, thrilling night.
With laughter ringing, hearts align,
In this rhythm, we intertwine.

Each whisper tells a tale anew,
As friendships blossom, pure and true.
Hand in hand, together we sway,
In the dance of life, come what may.

Let the music guide our way,
In the moment, let us stay.
For in these steps, we find our place,
In the dance of new encounters, grace.

Bonds Like Rivers

Flowing gently, side by side,
Bonds like rivers never hide.
Through the hills and valleys deep,
In their waters, secrets keep.

Winding paths of joy and strife,
In the current, flows our life.
Every twist, each turn we make,
Strengthens the bond, never to break.

Together we weather every storm,
In the flow, we find our form.
Through droughts and floods, we learn to bend,
For bonds like rivers have no end.

In peace or chaos, we shall find,
Harmony, entwined and kind.
Bound together, hearts ignite,
Creating rivers, pure delight.

Gathering Under Shared Stars

Underneath the endless skies,
We gather as the daylight dies.
Our voices rise, a tranquil hum,
As constellations call us home.

With stories spun from golden thread,
In shadows cast, our lineage spread.
We share our dreams and hopes anew,
Beneath the stars, a radiant view.

Each twinkle holds a memory bright,
Of laughter echoing through the night.
In this moment, hearts align,
Gathered close, our spirits shine.

Together we weave a tapestry,
Of bonds that time cannot decree.
As stardust flows from hands to hearts,
In this gathering, the magic starts.

Bridging the Distance

Across the miles, we reach for light,
Connecting our hearts, souls take flight.
Words like bridges, our voices strong,
In every silence, we still belong.

Though oceans part, spirits entwine,
Distance dissolves, love's design.
Stars align to guide our way,
In dreams, we meet, come what may.

A call in the night, a whisper shared,
In every echo, we've both cared.
Hand in hand, though far apart,
Every beat holds the other's heart.

Seasons will change, yet still we stay,
Painting our skies in shades of gray.
In every sunset, a promise made,
With courage, the distance will surely fade.

Through laughter, tears, we grow anew,
In this journey, me and you.
No matter the road that lies ahead,
Together we forge the path we tread.

The Symphony of Togetherness

In harmony, we share our song,
A melody where we both belong.
Each note, a thread, woven tight,
In the silence, hearts ignite.

Through ups and downs, we sway in time,
Building a rhythm, sweet and sublime.
Every measure, a dance we share,
In this symphony, love lays bare.

Chorus of laughter, a soft refrain,
Echoes of joy, through pleasure and pain.
In unity, we find our grace,
Together we blossom, in this space.

With instrumental dreams on the rise,
Together we see, through each other's eyes.
No discord can break what we compose,
In this orchestra, our love just grows.

As the final note begins to fade,
In every heart, our love is laid.
With every smile, a perfect tune,
In our symphony, forever in bloom.

Footprints in New Places

In uncharted lands, we take our walk,
Leaving behind whispers, words that talk.
With every step, a story unfolds,
Adventures waiting, as life beholds.

The earth beneath, a canvas vast,
Each footprint a memory, shadows cast.
Through valleys deep and mountains high,
Together we journey, just you and I.

With every sunrise, new paths arise,
Under the expanse of endless skies.
In foreign streets, we dance with grace,
Creating a bond, in this new place.

The compass spins, but hearts stay true,
Navigating dreams, just me and you.
In every corner, new joys await,
Together entwined, we forge our fate.

As sunsets paint the evening's glow,
Through lush horizons, our love will grow.
Footprints in sand, we leave them there,
In every journey, a reminder to care.

A Garden of New Faces

In the garden where wildflowers bloom,
New faces gather, dispelling gloom.
Each petal whispers secrets untold,
In this sanctuary, warmth unfolds.

With laughter shared and stories spun,
In every heart, a spark begun.
Together we water, tend the ground,
In this space, kinship is found.

As seasons shift, we grow in grace,
Embracing the change, a friendly face.
In the roots of kindness, we find our place,
Building a community, woven with grace.

Through the tapestry of shared delight,
In every shadow, we find the light.
With hands held tight, we nurture the dream,
In this vibrant garden, love's the theme.

So let's sow the seeds of hope and cheer,
In this lush haven, we gather near.
With hearts open wide, a beautiful chase,
In the garden of love, we'll find our space.

Threads of Laughter

In the warmth of shared smiles,
We find solace in the light,
Each chuckle adds a stitch,
Woven tight with pure delight.

With echoes of joy resounding,
We dance beneath the stars,
Glimmering moments surrounding,
Reminding us of who we are.

In playful whispers we connect,
The world fades into a blur,
Each joyous memory to protect,
A bond that will not defer.

Through the tapestry of time,
In laughter, we entwine,
Threads of joy so sublime,
Forever in hearts they shine.

As seasons shift and change,
Our laughter still remains,
A melody that won't estrange,
In every joy, it sustains.

Expanding Horizons

Beyond the edge of sight,
Where dreams take flight,
We reach for the vast unknown,
With courage, seeds are sown.

Mountains tall, rivers wide,
Adventure calls, a thrilling ride,
In every step, we grow,
Learning from the paths we sow.

Through valleys deep and skies so clear,
Possibilities draw near,
With every breath taken in,
We trust the journey will begin.

Hands held tight, hearts aligned,
Together our souls intertwined,
In unity, we explore,
Unraveling mysteries galore.

With every dawn that breaks anew,
Horizon stretches wide and true,
As we venture side by side,
In the vastness, we abide.

Kindred Spirits Gather

Underneath the ancient trees,
We gather close, hearts at ease,
Each story shared, a thread of gold,
Binding us as days unfold.

In the quiet of the night,
Our laughter dances with the light,
With open arms, we receive,
A warmth that we believe.

With eyes that shine, we see the truth,
In every wrinkle, in every youth,
Through kindness, we embrace,
Finding home in every place.

The ties that bind us, strong and true,
Kindred spirits, tried and true,
Together, we face what may come,
In this circle, we are home.

And as the night begins to wane,
We hold the magic, we sustain,
For every heart that gathers here,
Is a melody, pure and clear.

A Tapestry of Souls

In time's embrace, we intertwine,
Stories merge, histories align,
Each thread a life, a spark so bright,
Together, we weave through day and night.

In colors bold, in shades so deep,
Moments captured, memories to keep,
With hands outstretched, we find our way,
Creating beauty in the fray.

Through trials faced, and joys that swell,
Each woven tale, a tale to tell,
With every knot, our hearts expand,
Strength in unity, hand in hand.

As stars above begin to gleam,
We gather close, share the dream,
A tapestry rich, a story told,
In the threads of love, we are bold.

And as we stand, in silence shared,
A celebration of hearts laid bare,
In this grand weave, we find our role,
Together we are a tapestry of souls.

Unwritten Chapters

In silence whispers dreams unfold,
Pages waiting, tales untold.
Ink of hope on paper bright,
Each word a spark, igniting light.

Through shadows cast, a journey starts,
Lines drawn close, entwining hearts.
With every chance that we embrace,
New stories bloom in time and space.

The future calls, an open door,
Adventures wait on distant shore.
Together now, we weave our fate,
With every choice, we captivate.

Mistakes may come, but lessons stay,
In every chapter, find your way.
A quest for truth, both bold and wise,
In unwritten lines, our spirit flies.

So here we stand, ready to write,
With every dawn, a fresh new light.
Hand in hand, we take the leap,
In unwritten chapters, dreams we keep.

The Garden of Friendship

In the garden where laughter grows,
Blooming petals, a friendship shows.
Roots entwined beneath the ground,
In this haven, love is found.

Sunlight spills on every leaf,
Moments shared, beyond belief.
Nurtured hearts in gentle care,
In joy and sorrow, always there.

Colors blend in sweet delight,
With every laugh, we take to flight.
Through seasons change, our bond stays true,
In this garden, me and you.

When clouds appear, and shadows cast,
We face the storms, our friendship vast.
Each trial makes our roots grow deep,
In this garden, memories keep.

So let us tend this sacred space,
With tender hearts, and warm embrace.
In blooms we find our shared decree,
In the garden, forever free.

Beyond Boundaries

Across the seas, in distant lands,
A dream awaits in unseen strands.
With every heartbeat, courage calls,
To break the lines, to scale the walls.

Together strong, we take a stand,
A tapestry, both bright and grand.
With open minds, we bridge the gap,
In unity, we find our map.

Daring paths, where few have tread,
In stepping forth, all fears we shed.
With hands held high, reaching the sky,
Beyond boundaries, we learn to fly.

Voices rise, a chorus sweet,
In harmony, our worlds compete.
For every step, a story made,
In every heart, a bond displayed.

As stars align, we blend as one,
In every journey, new begun.
Together we forge, through rain or shine,
Beyond boundaries, your hand in mine.

Harmonies of the Heart

In gentle whispers, love awakes,
A melody that softly takes.
Each note a promise, sweetly sung,
In every heart, the song's begun.

With rhythms bold, we dance as two,
In every step, our spirits grew.
A symphony of dreams we've shared,
In every silence, love declared.

Through highs and lows, the music flows,
In every laugh, our essence glows.
With open arms, we find our place,
In this embrace, a warm embrace.

The chords of life, both rich and rare,
In harmony, we lay our care.
With every heartbeat, blend and sway,
In the song of us, we find our way.

So let us sing, with voices clear,
In this duet, year after year.
In harmonies of the heart so bright,
Together we'll soar, into the light.

Threads of Togetherness

In the fabric of life we weave,
Colors blend and hearts believe.
Each stitch a moment, softly sewn,
Together we shine, never alone.

With laughter shared, our spirits rise,
Through gentle whispers, we touch the skies.
In every tear and every smile,
Threads of love stretch every mile.

Hand in hand, we face the storm,
Creating warmth, a safe, bright form.
Our journeys twine, like rivers flow,
In strength of bond, together we grow.

Through trials faced, we hold so tight,
Guiding each other with hearts alight.
In the tapestry of cherished dreams,
Unity shines, or so it seems.

So let us cherish this sacred thread,
In the dance of life, where we are led.
For in togetherness, we truly find,
The beauty of love, forever intertwined.

The Dance of Companionship

Two souls unite in graceful sway,
Moving as one, come what may.
In every step, we find our beat,
Partners bound, our lives complete.

With every turn in this grand ballet,
Trust forms a path where hearts will play.
A waltz of joy, through highs and lows,
In this embrace, true love only grows.

The rhythm guides us, hand in hand,
Together we flow, as grains of sand.
With laughter's song and sorrow's tune,
We dance beneath the watchful moon.

Not just in ease, but through the strife,
We share the weight, this dance of life.
With every stumble, every fall,
Together we rise, we conquer all.

As seasons change and shadows cast,
Our dance endures, unwavering and fast.
In the melody of shared delight,
Companionship glows, our guiding light.

Radiant Bonds

In the warmth of friendship, hearts entwine,
Radiant bonds, a love divine.
Through laughter's glow and sorrow's haze,
We shine together, lighting the days.

With every secret, whispered near,
We build a fortress, a haven here.
In shared adventures, joy flows free,
Each moment cherished, you and me.

As stars align in the velvet night,
Our spirits soar, taking flight.
Through every challenge, every strife,
These radiant bonds enhance our life.

With open hearts, we face the new,
Creating memories, just us two.
In every smile, every cheer,
Our friendship blooms, forever dear.

So here we stand, hand in hand,
With radiant warmth, a glowing band.
In the tapestry of time that's spun,
Together we're strength, together we're one.

Embracing the Journey

Together we wander, side by side,
Embracing the journey, a thrilling ride.
With dreams in our hearts and hope in our eyes,
Each step an adventure, the world our prize.

Through mountains tall and valleys deep,
In laughter and silence, our memories keep.
Every path we traverse, every twist and turn,
In the light of our bond, we endlessly learn.

With courage ignited, we chase the dawn,
Hand in hand, we'll carry on.
For each challenge faced fortifies our core,
With love as our compass, we always explore.

In the beauty of moments, both big and small,
We find our strength in the rise and fall.
For as we journey, our hearts unite,
Embracing each chapter, day and night.

So let us rejoice in this wondrous quest,
In every heartbeat, in every breath.
Together we flourish, forever we steer,
Embracing the journey, with love sincere.

Ties That Bind Us

In shadows deep, we find our way,
Through laughter's light and silence gray.
With every step, we grow entwined,
Two souls as one, a love defined.

Through storms we stand, resilient, true,
Our hearts beat strong in all we do.
With healing words, we mend the fray,
Each gentle touch, a bond to stay.

In moments shared, both bright and bleak,
A whispered hope when words are weak.
Together forged in trials faced,
In unity, our fears displaced.

With unseen threads, we're drawn so near,
Each knot we tie, we hold most dear.
Embrace the strength of what we share,
Our spirits dance in honest care.

So let us weave our dreams anew,
With each connection, love shines through.
For in this life, it's plain to see,
The ties that bind enrich us free.

The Web We Weave

In twilight's hue, our fates align,
With gentle hands, we craft the sign.
Each thread we twist in love's embrace,
A tapestry of time and space.

Through whispers soft, our stories blend,
In laughter's glow, our hearts shall mend.
Invisible strands that tie us tight,
In darkness found, we seek the light.

With every stitch, a lesson learned,
In fire's warmth, our passions burned.
Our scars reflect the paths we've trod,
In tangled mess, a hint of God.

As seasons change and moments sway,
We gather strength from yesterday.
For in this web, both fierce and frail,
Together we shall always prevail.

So weave your dreams with threads of gold,
Embrace the tales yet to be told.
For life is but a dance we share,
In the web we weave, love fills the air.

Connections Unfurled

Like rivers flowing, hearts entwined,
In every glance, a spark designed.
With open arms, we reach for more,
Each bond we share, a cherished core.

In laughter's echo, joy will bloom,
Through whispered hopes, dispelling gloom.
Our paths converge like stars in night,
In silent vows, we hold on tight.

As seasons shift and days unfold,
Our stories weave, a thread of gold.
With gentle hearts, we nurture seeds,
In every act, a love that leads.

Through trials faced and dreams pursued,
We stand as one, with gratitude.
In every challenge, hand in hand,
A strength emerges, ever grand.

So let us rise, our spirits fly,
With every bond, we multiply.
Together forged, we'll face the world,
In every moment, connections unfurled.

Kinship in Bloom

In gardens rich, our roots run deep,
Where laughter flows and sorrows weep.
With petals bright, we share our grace,
A kinship blooms in warm embrace.

Through sunlit days and stormy nights,
We find our way, igniting lights.
In whispers shared, our fears take flight,
A tapestry of pure delight.

As seasons turn, we learn and grow,
With every step, our bond will show.
In gentle hues, our spirits blend,
In harmony, we start to mend.

With open hearts, we nurture dreams,
In brightened paths, our future beams.
Together strong, we'll face each test,
In kinship found, we feel the blessed.

So let us thrive in love's embrace,
In every moment, find our place.
For in this life where flowers bloom,
A kinship grows, dispelling gloom.

United Through Differences

We gather with minds, diverse and bright,
Each voice a story, a shared delight.
Embracing our past, our cultures unite,
Together we shine, in love's warm light.

In chaos we find, a rhythm true,
Differences blend, like morning dew.
Hand in hand, we're weaving anew,
A tapestry rich, with every hue.

Though paths may diverge, we stand side by side,
In the heart of the storm, we take each stride.
For strength lies within, where hope won't hide,
Together we flourish, as love is our guide.

With laughter that binds, and kindness that heals,
We nurture our dreams, with compassion's appeals.
In unity's grasp, our spirits reveal,
A future more bright, together it feels.

So raise up your voice, let harmony swell,
In differences found, our stories we tell.
For united we stand, and together we dwell,
In a world that is rich, where all hearts excel.

Colorful Connections

In gardens of thought, we blossom and grow,
Each petal a story, in vibrant show.
Unity blooms, where friendships flow,
Through the hues of our lives, together we glow.

A canvas of laughter, with colors we blend,
Each shade unique, yet together we mend.
In the arms of support, we find time to spend,
Crafting our dreams, hand in hand we transcend.

With every heartbeat, a symphony plays,
As we dance through the nights and wander the days.
Through the rain we discover, in light not in haze,
Connections that spark in mysterious ways.

We celebrate moments, small joys we receive,
In the tapestry woven, we learn to believe.
In the garden of life, hope blossoms and weaves,
Colorful connections, where love never leaves.

So let us embrace, this radiant thread,
In a world of colors, where every heart's fed.
Together we shine, with every word said,
In the beauty of friendship, our spirits are led.

Shadows of Support

In silence we stand, where shadows may play,
Offering comfort, when words fade away.
A gentle presence, to brighten the gray,
In shadows of support, we find our way.

Through trials we journey, hand in hand tight,
As whispers of hope warm the coldest of nights.
With strength in our hearts, we face every fight,
For together we're strong, in friendship's pure light.

When burdens grow heavy, and path seems unclear,
In shadows we gather, dispelling each fear.
With love as our shield, we draw ever near,
Together we flourish, as kind spirits cheer.

In moments of doubt, we stand as a wall,
In shadows of laughter, we rise, never fall.
For every small victory, we gather, we call,
In this dance of support, we share it with all.

So hold tight your dreams, don't let them slip past,
In the shadows of life, our bond will hold fast.
For through every struggle, together we'll last,
In a world of support, our shadows hold fast.

The Journey of Many Steps

With each step we take, a story unfolds,
In the dance of our lives, the future it molds.
Paths may be winding, with treasures untold,
The journey of many steps, brave and bold.

Through valleys of doubt, and mountains of hope,
We navigate life, learning how to cope.
With each footfall forward, new dreams we elope,
In the journey of many steps, we find our scope.

We cherish the moments, both silent and loud,
As we walk together, a united crowd.
In our hearts beats the rhythm, steady and proud,
In this journey of many steps, we wear our shroud.

As seasons will change, and time marches on,
With each sunrise breaking, a new day reborn.
Embracing the path, through every dawn,
In the journey of many steps, together we're drawn.

So let us step forth, with courage and grace,
In the journey of many steps, we find our place.
With love as our compass, in this vast space,
Together we journey, our hearts interlace.

Tapestry of Memories

Threads of laughter weave the past,
In shadows where our dreams are cast.
Colors blend, both bright and pale,
Stories linger in every trail.

Moments crafted, time unfolds,
In gentle whispers, secrets told.
Each stitch a heartbeat, feelings strong,
Together we dance, our hearts belong.

Golden sunsets, mornings bright,
Captured in the fading light.
Echoes linger, soft and clear,
A tapestry of love held dear.

Faded photographs, worn and torn,
Memories cherished since the dawn.
In every corner, joy resides,
A woven bond that never hides.

Through the years, we'll find our way,
In this tapestry, come what may.
Each thread a story, interlace,
In the fabric of our shared grace.

Wings of Camaraderie

Through the skies we rise and soar,
Side by side, forevermore.
Gentle breezes guide our flight,
In unity, we chase the light.

Feathers ruffled, spirits high,
Together we reach for the sky.
With open hearts, we take the leap,
In laughter shared, our bond runs deep.

We gather strength from roots below,
In storms of life, together grow.
With wings outstretched, we find our song,
In every note, we all belong.

In every journey, hand in hand,
We carve our path, we make our stand.
Like birds in flight, we navigate,
With camaraderie, we celebrate.

As the sun sets, our shadows blend,
In this flight, we find a friend.
For every ending spurs new wings,
Together, we embrace what life brings.

The Embrace of Many

In circles wide, we gather near,
Voices meld, a chorus clear.
Hands entwined, a solid bond,
In unity, we forge beyond.

Each heartbeat echoes, strong and bold,
In stories shared, our hearts unfold.
Together we stand, no one alone,
In every embrace, true love is sown.

Diverse in spirit, kind in heart,
Every soul plays a vital part.
With open arms, we weather storms,
In the embrace of many, love warms.

As seasons change, we'll stand as one,
With laughter shared and battles won.
No shadows cast can dim our flame,
In every way, we are the same.

Through trials faced, and joys displayed,
In every spirit, love conveyed.
Together we rise, a mighty throng,
In the embrace of many, we belong.

Building Bridges

In every heart, a bridge we make,
Connecting souls for friendship's sake.
With gentle words, we span the gap,
In every gesture, no time to nap.

Brick by brick, we lay our trust,
In shared laughter, it's a must.
With open arms, we reach across,
In unity found, we never lose.

Through rivers wide and mountains tall,
Together we'll answer the call.
With sturdy beams, our bonds unite,
In every challenge, we share the light.

As seasons shift, our focus stays,
In every bridge, we'll find new ways.
To traverse the highs and lows,
With love as the path, our journey flows.

Through storms we stand, bridge in hand,
Creating pathways, strong and grand.
In every step, we'll strive to show,
Building bridges, together we grow.

Heartstrings Intertwined

In the silence, our hearts meet,
Whispers soft, a rhythmic beat.
Like vines that twist and gently bind,
Two souls in dance, perfectly aligned.

Through storms and sun, we hold on tight,
In shadows cast, we find the light.
With every glance, our worlds collide,
In this embrace, we take each stride.

The fabric woven, threads of fate,
Each stitch a promise, love innate.
In laughter shared and tears we've wept,
Through every moment, love we've kept.

As seasons change, our roots grow deep,
In the garden of love, we sow and reap.
Together we rise, together we fall,
In the tapestry of life, we give our all.

With heartstrings intertwined, we soar,
In this symphony, forevermore.
Through life's embrace, hand in hand,
Our love, a journey, beautifully planned.

Circling Joy

In the circle of laughter, we share,
Moments fleeting, light as air.
With every smile, our spirits gleam,
Boundless joy, like a waking dream.

Under the stars, we chase the night,
In each other's eyes, pure delight.
Dancing freely, hearts unconfined,
In this embrace, true joy we find.

The world spins softly, time holds still,
In this moment, we feel the thrill.
Whirling together, passion ignites,
As we chase the dawn with endless sights.

Through laughter's echo, our spirits sing,
In the harmony of love, we take wing.
With every heartbeat, the joy expands,
Holding tightly, we make our plans.

In circling joy, our souls entwined,
With open hearts, we seek and find.
As the sun rises, we greet the day,
In love's embrace, we'll forever stay.

Seeds of Affection

In the quiet earth, we plant our dreams,
Nurtured by love, the sunlight beams.
With tender care, we watch them grow,
Roots spreading wide, in hearts they show.

Through seasons' change, our bond takes flight,
In every hue, our love ignites.
With gentle hands, we tend the soil,
Harvesting joy from each sweet toil.

In the garden of hope, blossoms bloom,
Fragrance of love dispels the gloom.
As petals open, colors unfold,
Stories of affection silently told.

With every raindrop, a promise sown,
In the heart of love, we have grown.
Together we thrive, side by side,
In the tapestry of life, we abide.

In the seeds of affection, we believe,
With every heartbeat, we receive.
In the warmth of love, we find our place,
Together forever, in sweet embrace.

Echoes of Laughter

In the echoes of laughter, joy resounds,
Lingering softly, where love abounds.
With every giggle, the world comes alive,
In each shared moment, our spirits thrive.

Through echoes that dance, memories spin,
In the heart's chamber, where laughter begins.
With every chuckle, the shadows flee,
In this melody, we find harmony.

In playful banter, our hearts take flight,
Casting aside the dark of night.
With echoes ringing, our souls connect,
In this joyful sound, we find respect.

In the symphony of voices, we unite,
In laughter's embrace, all feels right.
With every shared joy, our bond grows strong,
In the echoes of laughter, we belong.

As time flows gently, and seasons change,
In the echoes of laughter, we rearrange.
Through life's adventures, one thing stays clear,
In love's sweet laughter, we hold dear.

Embracing New Horizons

In golden dawn, the sun appears,
A world anew, banishing fears.
With open hearts, we take the leap,
To chase the dreams that we dare keep.

The path may twist, the skies may gray,
Yet still we strive, come what may.
With every step, a chance to grow,
Unlocking doors to all we know.

So let us dance beneath the light,
Embracing change, our spirits bright.
Together we shall brave the tides,
With hope and love as our guides.

Through valleys deep, over hills high,
We lift our gaze, we aim for the sky.
A journey shared, each moment dear,
In every heartbeat, we find cheer.

The future calls, it's ours to mold,
With courage strong and dreams bold.
Together we will write the song,
Of new horizons, where we belong.

Radiance in Togetherness

In the glow of a shared embrace,
We find our home, our safest place.
With laughter bright, we light the way,
Together here, we choose to stay.

Each heart a spark, a flame aglow,
In unity, our spirits grow.
With gentle words and kindness shared,
A bond unbroken, love declared.

Through storms we face, we stand as one,
With every trial, our strength begun.
In silent whispers, our hopes collide,
In this sweet haven, we abide.

With arms outstretched, horizons near,
We celebrate, no room for fear.
In every challenge, we find a way,
Together, we shall seize the day.

Radiant hearts, united we shine,
In every moment, your hand in mine.
Through thick and thin, our spirits soar,
In love and laughter, forevermore.

Ripples of Influence

A single touch, a gentle wave,
The power flows, the hearts we save.
In kindness shared, we plant the seeds,
Of hope that blooms and loving deeds.

With every word, a stone is cast,
Creating waves that long will last.
In actions small, the world we change,
Through simple gestures, hearts arrange.

The ripples spread, beyond our sight,
As love takes flight, igniting light.
In quiet moments, we intertwine,
Our souls connected, bright and fine.

From distant shores, they echo back,
The ties we weave, the joy we track.
For every kindness, sparks ignite,
Together, we can change the night.

In every heart, influence grows,
A dance of love, as nature shows.
Through vibrant waves, our spirits glide,
In unity, we stand with pride.

Threads of Joy

In tapestry of dreams we weave,
Threads of joy, we shall believe.
Each vibrant hue, a story told,
Of laughter shared, and hearts of gold.

With gentle hands, we stitch with care,
A world of hope, beyond compare.
In every knot, a bond so tight,
In shared delight, our hearts take flight.

Through sunny days and stormy nights,
Together we create the lights.
With every twist, our paths align,
In threads of joy, our spirits shine.

Each moment shared, a memory spun,
In love's embrace, we have begun.
With laughter rich and stories deep,
In threads of joy, our souls we keep.

So let us weave with hearts so true,
A tapestry of me and you.
In every thread, a love that flows,
In joyous hues, together grows.

The Mosaic of Unity

From shards of glass we come together,
Each piece reflects a light,
In colors bright, we stand as one,
Creating beauty, day and night.

With voices raised, we share our song,
In harmony, our spirits soar,
Each note a thread, a bond so strong,
In this embrace, we seek for more.

Differences we celebrate,
In every shape, in every hue,
A tapestry of love we create,
For in our hearts, we're kind and true.

Together building bridges wide,
Over rivers of despair,
In unity, we take this stride,
With care and love, our souls laid bare.

A mosaic bright, we shine and glow,
Each story told, a vital part,
In every corner, kindness flows,
The mosaic lives within our heart.

Unfolding Adventures

Beneath the stars, we chart our course,
With dreams aflame, we seek the new,
Each moment brings its own sweet force,
Guiding us where skies are blue.

With every step, the world unfolds,
A canvas vast and full of grace,
In whispered tales, the future holds,
A path for those who dare to pace.

On mountain tops and ocean shores,
The thrill of life ignites our hearts,
As we explore what nature pours,
In every dawn, a new day starts.

Through valleys deep, and forests wide,
We dance with winds, embrace the rain,
In shared laughter, our fears subside,
Adventure calls, we rise, unchained.

So let us wander, hand in hand,
Where magic lives in every light,
For in each journey, we will stand,
Unfolding dreams, our spirits bright.

Hands Across Time

In gentle grasp, our stories blend,
A thread through ages, strong and fine,
With every touch, the past we mend,
United through the sands of time.

With ancient echoes in our soul,
We carry wisdom, passed along,
In whispers soft, we feel the whole,
A timeless glow, a sacred song.

Together, we build bridges wide,
With love as mortar, strong and true,
Across the years, with hearts as guide,
We find our way, in all we do.

Each hand we hold, a beacon bright,
Illuminating paths unknown,
Through every struggle, every fight,
In unity, we have grown.

So let us stand, our differences few,
In harmony, we'll weave our fate,
For hands across time will renew,
A legacy that will not wait.

A Network of Kindness

In every smile, a spark ignites,
A web of love connects our hearts,
Through gentle words and shining lights,
A network grows, as kindness starts.

With open arms, we share our cares,
In moments shared, our spirits rise,
Together, we are the answer to prayers,
A tapestry of hope that ties.

In acts of grace, our hearts reflect,
The beauty found in giving free,
With every touch, we reconnect,
A bond of warmth, a shared decree.

Through storms of life, we'll stand as one,
In unity, we'll find our way,
For every deed that we have done,
Creates a brighter, kinder day.

So let us weave this cherished thread,
A network strong, forever true,
With kindness in the words we've said,
A world transformed, with love anew.

A Symphony of Souls

In the quiet dusk we meet,
Notes of laughter fill the air.
Hearts in rhythm, souls in beat,
Weaving moments, rich and rare.

Every glance a story told,
Whispers echoing through the night.
In your eyes, the warmth of gold,
A symphony of pure delight.

Melodies of joy arise,
Dancing shadows on the floor.
With each harmony, we fly,
Together, forevermore.

Softly played, the world aligns,
In the embrace of this sweet song.
Fingers touch, and light entwines,
In this place where we belong.

Let's compose a dream so wide,
In the light of starlit skies.
In this journey, hearts our guide,
Together, as the spirit flies.

The Roots of Togetherness

In the garden, hand in hand,
Seeds of trust begin to grow.
Through each heart, a silent strand,
Ties that bind and softly flow.

Echoes of our laughter ring,
Shared moments, sunlight bright.
In this space, love's offering,
Sprouts of hope take root in light.

Through the storms, we bravely stand,
Held by stories, old and new.
In unity, we make our plan,
Nurtured by the love we brew.

With every step, we intertwine,
Branches stretching toward the sun.
In this bond, our lives align,
Together, we become as one.

Roots that dig into the earth,
Growing deeper, strong, and free.
In our hearts, we find our worth,
Together, just you and me.

A Voyage Through Time

Upon the sea of memories,
Waves of laughter, whispers blend.
Sailing forth on gentle breeze,
Each moment, a trusted friend.

Through the ages, stories flow,
Fragments of a life lived well.
In the tides, we ebb and glow,
Every tale, a fleeting spell.

Stars above, our guiding light,
Bringing hope through darkest nights.
In our hearts, the fire bright,
Navigating endless sights.

Time, a river, fierce and wide,
Carries dreams on currents strong.
In this voyage, side by side,
Where we've been, where we belong.

As the dawn begins to rise,
We will chart the course ahead.
With open hearts and eager eyes,
Together, dreams to be spread.

Connections Across Landscapes

In the valleys and the hills,
Voices travel, hearts unite.
Every journey, passion spills,
In the morning's golden light.

Mountains echo with our dreams,
Rivers carry tales untold.
In the stillness, hope redeems,
Stories shared, though hearts are bold.

Through the forests, wild and deep,
Nature weaves our spirits' thread.
In the silence, secrets seep,
Connections made where paths are led.

Far horizons call our names,
In the distance, dreams alight.
Every heartbeat fuels the flames,
As we walk, souls take flight.

Through the storm and through the calm,
Hand in hand, we find our way.
In the night, a soothing balm,
Together, come what may.

Kinship Beyond Borders

Across the seas, our hearts align,
In every smile, our stories shine.
Bound by love, yet apart we stand,
Unity speaks through a gentle hand.

No matter the distance, we share a song,
In whispered dreams, we all belong.
Cultures blend like colors bright,
Together we dance, a shared delight.

From mountains high to valleys deep,
In every promise, our secrets keep.
Fingers entwined, we bridge the divide,
In kinship's warmth, we take great pride.

Through trials faced, we rise as one,
In laughter's light, our battles won.
We build a world, hand-in-hand,
In love's embrace, forever we stand.

So here's to bonds that never fade,
In every heart, a lasting trade.
Together we'll write history's page,
In kinship's glow, we share our stage.

Together We Blossom

In gardens lush, where hope takes flight,
We sow our dreams, beneath the light.
With tender care, our roots entwine,
In every bloom, our spirits shine.

Through seasons changing, hand in hand,
We weather storms, we understand.
With every petal, a tale to tell,
United we rise, we break the shell.

In vibrant hues, our voices blend,
Through laughter shared, we find a friend.
Together we nurture, together we grow,
In harmony's dance, our love will show.

As sunlight fades, the stars ablaze,
In twilight's whisper, we find our ways.
Each fragrant moment, each tender sigh,
In this sweet garden, forever we'll fly.

So here's to all the paths we tread,
In blossom's embrace, where dreams are fed.
Together we rise, through joy and strife,
In this wondrous journey, we share our life.

Beyond the Familiar

In lands unknown, we seek and roam,
With open hearts, we find a home.
Through winding roads, our spirits soar,
In every face, a world to explore.

Beneath new skies, we find our way,
Every sunset, a brand new day.
With stories shared under starlit skies,
Through every tear, a bond that ties.

In cultures rich, we learn and grow,
Embracing differences, the beauty flows.
In laughter's light, connection is found,
In every heartbeat, love knows no bound.

With every journey, a lesson learned,
Through paths untraveled, our souls have yearned.
Together we wander, hand in hand,
In the tapestry of life, we understand.

So here's to adventures that lie ahead,
In worlds we paint, where none have tread.
Together we'll forge a brighter dawn,
In unity's embrace, we'll carry on.

Harmony in Different Voices

From every corner, a tale unfolds,
In varied tongues, our destiny holds.
With open hearts, we gather near,
In every story, we face our fear.

Each note distinct, yet bound in song,
In differing shades, we all belong.
Through the rhythms of life, we find our way,
In harmony's beauty, we learn to sway.

Voices rising like a symphony,
Each note a thread in our tapestry.
With love as our guide, we break the mold,
In every chord, our truths unfold.

As stars align in the midnight sky,
With hope in our hearts, we aim to fly.
Through valleys low and mountains high,
United, we soar, together we try.

So here's to the chorus that makes us whole,
In differences shared, we find our role.
Together we sing, the world will hear,
In harmony's embrace, we conquer fear.

Unity in Diversity

In colors bright we stand together,
Each shade a story, each voice a tether.
Hand in hand through storm and light,
Different paths, yet spirits unite.

Embracing cultures, we learn and grow,
In every heart, a seed will sow.
Dancing in rhythm, feeling the beat,
Unity shines when we all meet.

Differences cherished, not pushed aside,
Strength in our bonds, with love as our guide.
Together we rise, break every wall,
In the tapestry of life, we are all.

Voices harmonize, a beautiful song,
In diversity, we all belong.
Each life's journey, a shared refrain,
In unity's embrace, we find no pain.

So let us celebrate every hue,
In this grand mosaic, me and you.
Together we stand, hearts open wide,
In unity's arms, we take pride.

The Spark of Connection

A glance, a smile, the start of flame,
In a world so vast, we're all the same.
A spark ignites in the still of night,
In every heart, there's a guiding light.

Words unspoken, yet understood,
Emotions blooming, bright and good.
Through shared laughter and gentle tears,
Connections flourish, cast away fears.

Each moment shared, a treasure we keep,
In this tapestry of life, we leap.
A touch, a whisper, bonds intertwine,
In the heart's garden, love's vines align.

In fleeting seconds, histories blend,
Each connection holds the power to mend.
Through every heartbeat, through every sigh,
We find our home as the days go by.

So cherish the spark, let it grow bright,
In every soul, discover the light.
For in this dance, we all play a part,
A beautiful union, heart to heart.

Kindred Hearts in Motion

Two souls collide on this winding road,
With every step, a story bestowed.
In laughter and tears, we learn and thrive,
Together we flourish, fully alive.

With open arms, we face the storm,
In kindred spirits, we find our norm.
Through shifting sands and changing skies,
In our hearts, a bond never dies.

As journeys unfold, hand in hand we roam,
Creating memories that feel like home.
Through mountains high and valleys wide,
In every heartbeat, walks side by side.

With dreams that soar and hopes that gleam,
We chase the echoes of a common dream.
Together we dance, through night and day,
In the warmth of friendship, we find our way.

So here's to the moments, both big and small,
In this beautiful journey, together we fall.
For kindred hearts, forever embrace,
In the rhythm of love, we find our place.

Journeys Together

Across the land, on paths untold,
We walk together, both brave and bold.
In every step, new stories rise,
With every sunrise, a sweet surprise.

Through fields of green and skies of blue,
In shared adventures, we start anew.
With hearts wide open, we take the chance,
In laughter and joy, we share our dance.

The road may twist, the trail may veer,
But side by side, we face our fear.
In moments of silence, our souls speak clear,
In the journey of life, we hold each dear.

Through trials and triumphs, side by side,
In the bonds we build, our hopes collide.
With each moment cherished, we grow and learn,
In the fire of friendship, our passions burn.

So here's to the journeys, both near and far,
With every heartbeat, a guiding star.
In this beautiful voyage, together we sail,
In the map of our lives, love will prevail.

Seeds of Understanding

In the garden of thought, we plant our dreams,
With seeds of wisdom, flowing like streams.
Each word a petal, soft and bright,
We nurture our minds, day and night.

Roots stretch deep, in soil so rich,
Learning unfolds, no single hitch.
Together we grow, in sun and rain,
Creating a tapestry, joy and pain.

With patience we wait, for flowers to bloom,
The fragrance of knowledge fills the room.
Hand in hand, we share our fate,
Building a future, we'll cultivate.

As seasons change, our journey flows,
In every setback, a lesson grows.
Through storms we bend, but do not break,
With every challenge, new paths we make.

In the end, together we stand,
Hearts united, a loving band.
With seeds we've sown, our spirits soar,
In the garden of life, we bloom evermore.

Constellations of Companions

In the velvet night, we gather close,
Under stars that twinkle, we share the most.
Each light a story, of laughter and tears,
In the constellation of hopes and fears.

Together we wander, through time and space,
Drawing connections, our hearts embrace.
The universe wide, yet we find our place,
In the dance of companions, each a grace.

Across the heavens, our dreams align,
Guided by starlight, a path so fine.
Through dark and light, our spirits shine,
In every heartbeat, your love is mine.

We map our journey, with laughter and care,
Finding solace in moments we share.
Through trials faced, we rise and fall,
In each other's strength, we conquer all.

With every dawn, our friendship grows,
Like constellations, forever it glows.
In unity forged, we'll find our way,
Through every night, into the day.

Intertwined Paths

Two paths crossed, fate intertwined,
In the forest of life, our hearts aligned.
Through winding trails, we journey on,
With every step, a new dawn's song.

The whispers of trees guide our way,
In shadows and light, together we sway.
With hands held tight, we conquer the climb,
In the rhythm of love, that knows no time.

As seasons shift, and rivers flow,
In the fabric of life, our colors glow.
Each moment cherished, each laugh a gift,
In the dance of existence, our spirits lift.

Through storms we weather, together we stand,
In the tapestry woven, you understand.
With trust unbroken, we face the test,
In the heart of the journey, we find our best.

And when the paths blur, as they might,
In the bonds we share, we'll find the light.
For every step on this road we trace,
Together we'll flourish, in love's embrace.

Notes of Nurturing

A gentle whisper, a loving tone,
In the song of life, we're never alone.
Each note a promise, held deep inside,
With nurturing hearts, we take the ride.

In the symphony of trust, we play,
With chords of kindness, guiding the way.
A melody sweet, in laughter we find,
The beauty of moments, joy intertwined.

Harmonies blend, as we rise and fall,
In the notes shared, we answer the call.
With every heartbeat, the rhythm flows,
In nurturing love, our spirit glows.

Through trials faced, we find our grace,
In the music of life, we find our place.
Each struggle a lesson, every tear a song,
Together we journey, where we belong.

So let us sing, with voices so clear,
In the notes of nurturing, we hold dear.
With every word, we plant the seed,
In the garden of hope, our hearts are freed.

Through Shared Lenses

In distant lands, we find our way,
Two souls converge, come what may.
A glance can spark a shared delight,
Connecting hearts in the soft twilight.

Through whispered words, we share our dreams,
In each other's eyes, the world redeems.
Moments captured, forever bold,
A tale of friendship, woven and told.

With every laugh, we break the mold,
A bond that warms, a hand to hold.
Our stories merge like rivers flow,
In unity, together we grow.

The colors fade, yet still we see,
The beauty found in harmony.
A canvas bright, our spirits dance,
Through shared lenses, we find our chance.

In shadows deep, we find the light,
A journey shared, our hearts ignite.
Each moment cherished, fiercely true,
Through shared lenses, I see you.

A Landscape of Connection

Mountains rise, horizons blend,
In nature's arms, two hearts extend.
We walk the paths that intertwine,
A landscape rich, your hand in mine.

The gentle breeze stirs memories deep,
In silence shared, our secrets keep.
With every step, we weave our fate,
A tapestry where love creates.

In fields of gold, we laugh and play,
Moments bloom, and time slips away.
With every heartbeat, shadows fade,
In this vast land, our dreams are laid.

Sunrise whispers of hopes anew,
In every dawn, I'm drawn to you.
A landscape vast, yet close we stand,
Connected souls in this enchanted land.

The stars above guide our way,
Through darkened nights, we find our day.
In every sigh, in every glance,
A landscape of connection, our sweet chance.

Reflections in Each Other

In quiet pools, we find our face,
Mirrored whispers, a gentle embrace.
The depths reveal what eyes can't see,
Reflections bloom, just you and me.

In laughter shared, our echoes ring,
In sorrow's fall, we learn to sing.
With every tear, we craft our art,
Reflections blend within the heart.

The light you bring illuminates,
Each shadow fades; love resonates.
In every doubt, a guiding spark,
Reflections bloom within the dark.

We walk a path that knows no end,
In every curve, we find our friend.
With every glance, our spirits soar,
Reflections of love forevermore.

In stillness found, we learn to trust,
In every moment, a sacred gust.
Together we stand, forever true,
Reflections in each other, me and you.

The Bridges We Build

With every word, we span the gap,
A bridge of trust in friendship's map.
Together we traverse the night,
In shadows cast, we find the light.

The beams of hope extend so wide,
In unity, we stand with pride.
With laughter rich, the ties are sealed,
Through every struggle, love revealed.

In storms that rage, we anchor fast,
A bond that weaves, forever cast.
Across the chasms, hand in hand,
The bridges built, together we stand.

Through valleys low and peaks that rise,
The heart knows well where friendship lies.
With every step, we chase the thrill,
Creating paths that time can't kill.

In gentle whispers, secrets shared,
Through every chapter, love declared.
The bridges we build, a timeless art,
Connecting souls, heart to heart.

Bonds Beyond Borders

In distant lands, we find our kin,
A bond that holds, despite the din.
Cultures blend, hearts intertwine,
Together we shine, through space and time.

Words may differ, but smiles are clear,
Friendship grows, year after year.
Through valleys low and mountains high,
Side by side, we reach the sky.

In every hug a story lives,
In every laugh, the heart forgives.
Though miles apart, we stand as one,
A tapestry woven, never undone.

From every corner, tales arise,
In unity, our spirits rise.
Bound by love, we learn and grow,
A river deep, a gentle flow.

No walls can break what we hold true,
In every heartbeat, I find you.
Together now, we pave the way,
To brighter nights and hopeful days.

Portraits of Laughter

In snapshots bright, our laughter sings,
Moments captured, joy it brings.
With every grin, the world feels light,
Painted smiles in golden light.

Tickled hearts and playful sighs,
In every glance, a sweet surprise.
Through shared stories, our colors blend,
Creating warmth that will not end.

From silly games to late-night chats,
We build our dreams on friendly pats.
Every chuckle, a frame in time,
In this gallery, love will climb.

Unscripted moments, bright and bold,
These cherished tales will never grow old.
Side by side, we paint our days,
In hues of joy, in laughter's rays.

As portraits live on every wall,
Our laughter echoes, a timeless call.
In heart and soul, we'll always play,
In laughter's warmth, we find our way.

Feelings of Belonging

In every glance, a home is found,
In every heart, a loving sound.
Together here, we stand so tall,
In unity, we break down walls.

With every story shared with grace,
We weave a bond, a sacred space.
Through laughter's thread and whispered dreams,
A chorus strong, or so it seems.

Hand in hand, through thick and thin,
In this journey, we all win.
The warmth of friendship, ever near,
A shelter built from love and cheer.

In every moment, we embrace,
In every heartbeat, a soft place.
Together, we find our sacred song,
In this symphony, we all belong.

With arms wide open, come what may,
We'll share our dreams, come join the play.
In this circle, we feel the call,
In feelings of belonging, we rise, we fall.

Tidal Waves of Friendship

Like waves that crash upon the shore,
Friendship builds and evermore.
In every tide, a strength we find,
With open hearts, and open minds.

Through seasons change, we ebb and flow,
In laughter's tide, our spirits grow.
From whispered words to roaring cheers,
We stand together, face our fears.

In every splash, we find our sense,
A bond so deep, it feels immense.
Through storms we sail, through calm we bask,
In friendship's glow, we need not ask.

With every crest, we rise so high,
In friendship's light, we learn to fly.
The ocean vast, yet shores so near,
Together we conquer, persevere.

So let the waves roll in and out,
For in this journey, there's no doubt.
Tidal waves of friendship, strong and true,
In every heartbeat, it's me and you.

Welcoming the Unknown

In shadows deep, a whisper calls,
Through hidden paths beyond the walls.
With open hearts, we step ahead,
Embracing dreams that gently spread.

The stars align, a map unfurls,
Guiding us through unseen worlds.
With every breath, we taste the new,
In every dawn, horizons too.

The fear of what tomorrow brings,
Transforms to hope as freedom sings.
We hold the light, we walk its grace,
Together we find a sacred space.

So let us leap, and trust the flight,
Into the arms of endless night.
With courage sewn in every seam,
We welcome in the wildest dream.

Celebrating Togetherness

In laughter's glow, our spirits rise,
A tapestry of joyous ties.
With hands entwined, we share this day,
In every hug, love finds its way.

Around the table, stories flow,
In every glance, the warmth we show.
The bonds we weave, a vibrant thread,
A quilt of joy, where hearts are fed.

With every cheer, a memory made,
In every dance, our fears cascade.
Through times of joy, through times of tears,
Together we conquer all our fears.

So let us raise a toast anew,
To friendships deep that ever grew.
In every moment, let us see,
The beauty found in you and me.

Ties Beyond Time

In quiet whispers, hearts align,
Through lifetimes vast, a sacred sign.
No distance, space, or time can break,
The bonds we hold, the love we make.

Through changing seasons, we remain,
In sun and shadow, joy and pain.
A thread unspooled, yet tightly spun,
In every battle, we have won.

In laughter shared, in silence known,
In every seed of love we've sown.
The stories old, the dreams unclosed,
In all our journeys, we have grown.

So though the years may drift away,
In heart and soul, we choose to stay.
Forever tied, eternally,
Through time and space, just you and me.

New Chapters

With every dawn, a page turned bright,
In stories old, we find the light.
With every choice, a path we tread,
In scribbled lines, our dreams are spread.

Each chapter new, with lessons learned,
With all the bridges we have burned.
In every tear, a glimpse of grace,
Through every challenge, we find our place.

With open hearts, we write once more,
The tale of hopes and dreams in store.
In whispers sweet, our voices blend,
The journey's magic never ends.

So let us dream and let us dare,
In every breath, we choose to care.
In ink and love, our lives entwined,
With every chapter, joy defined.

Old Friends

In twilight's hue, in amber light,
Our laughter echoes, pure delight.
With stories shared, and memories spun,
In every heart, we are as one.

Through years that passed, through tears and smiles,
In every mile, we've forged our styles.
With open arms, we gather near,
In moments dear, we shed our fear.

With every glance, a word unsaid,
In silent bonds, our hearts are led.
Through all that's changed, we still remain,
In friendship's song, a sweet refrain.

So let us cherish all we share,
In every hug, a love laid bare.
Old friends, like roots, grow side by side,
In every moment, joy and pride.